The Works

Very Occasional Verse

revised and completed

Richard Waterhouse

To those, present or departed, for whose amusement (and mine) most of these pieces were written.

CONTENTS

INTRODUCTION

These not very numerous verses were written intermittently during a period of almost seventy years. Hence my choice of general title for them, although one or two do in fact mark a particular event.

Several may benefit from a word of explanation. Really just a largish mound, Muckleburgh is none the less the nearest thing to a proper hill on what used to be our part of the North Norfolk coast, so I thought it deserved a passing nod. 'Serenity' was inspired by a series of greetings cards that showed a pair of traditionally shaped but otherwise almost featureless hearts in various affectionate situations.

With 'All You Need is Rhythm' the trick is to find a pleasantly rhythmic way of reading out each sometimes discontinuous line of digits and likewise the irregularly stressed line with which it forms a couplet. Daisy was one of Dorothy's pet hamsters, which, when it died, I buried in the garden close to another that had predeceased it. Erato is, of course, the Muse of love poetry. The title of the verse celebrating County Wexford's phallic gateposts also refers to its success in a hurling competition.

My source of inspiration for 'Restricted Area' was a repeating pattern of angels and fiends on a wallpaper design displayed at Standen, the house near East Grinstead designed by Philip Webb and now owned by the National Trust. It was a greetings card with a repeating pattern of little stylised butterflies that prompted me to write 'The Horny Lepidopterist'. Louis Armstrong recorded Stomp off, Let's go with Erskine Tate's Vendome Orchestra in 1926. Walter is the mysterious Victorian whose fluctuating private income enabled him to devote most of his life to sex – mainly with numerous female prostitutes. He described and commented on many of these encounters in his extensive memoirs, but he has not yet been convincingly identified.

The last couplet of my most recent piece could, I suppose, be taken to imply that I condone the behaviour of irresponsible men. I don't. But I do admire women who are realists when it comes to their dealings with such men.

Nothing here is intended to cause hurt. All the included pieces were written to amuse myself and usually one other – though not always the same – person. They are arranged in very roughly chronological order.

A Young Rake's Creed

If love were for ever,
I should want none of it,
Because I could never
Have more than one of it.

Love
May come from above.
But love eternal
Is certainly infernal.

Alchemy

The force that fashioned us prepared its plan
With more concern for tidiness than tact,
Positioning in woman as in man
The organs appertaining to the act
Of love where, witnesses to doubtful taste,
They merge with those for ridding us of waste.

This indiscretion generated stress:
Ambivalence that shades into disgust.
Some shun coition as uncleanliness,
In some pollution even kindles lust,
While others find their bleak solution lies
Within a cage of joyless compromise.

Such people may regard our special link
Of love as sheer defilement, but not I,
Who, though not free from inhibition, think
The outcome elevates the means, which by
Their occult action mysteries unfold
Transmuting common metals into gold.

To you, my love, these lines may seem to be
A pompous and obscure defence of what
Presents no problems, in as much as we
Delight in it. Agreed; so let us not
Pursue the matter, but rejoice in this
Alchemical enhancement of our bliss.

Muckleburgh Hill

Twas right there I popped Elsie the question,
On the top of yon Muckleburgh Hill.
First she looked out to sea,
And then, turning to me,
She said quietly, 'Dearest, I will.'

Since last spring in the peace of the churchyard
Neath the turf she has lain cold and still.
But till I pass away,
I'll remember that day
With my Elsie on Muckleburgh Hill.

Anna in Glandford Churchyard

She raced around this boarding-point
For paradise or hell.
Perhaps her thoughts rose heavenwards,
But then her knickers fell.

Serenity

Cosily bedded,
Two loving hearts.
Tranquilly wedded;
No naughty parts.

All You Need is Rhythm

1   2   1 2 3
What's the matter, dummy? Why you starin' at me?

1   2   3   4
Go see to them drapes, an' you'd better lock the door.

1   2   3 4 5
What you up to there? Oh! Not again. Snakes alive!

1 2 3   4 5 6
Get your hands off my butt. I don't like dirty tricks.

1 2 3 4 5 6 7
If I says 'Yes' now, I'll never go to heaven.

1 2 3 4 5   6 7 8
I wanna go to heaven, but I jus' can't wait.

1 2 3 4 5 6 7 8 9
Now don't lose your cool, when you's doin' real fine.

Jus' keep on rock 'n' rollin',
An' we'll both arrive at 10.
Then chill out for a moment,
Till it's time to start again.

Daisy's Message for Dorothy

Affectionate and tender-hearted
Mistress, please don't cry for me.
Even though I've now departed,
Keep your spirits high for me.

Think of it as if I'd only
Gone to join a friend who's lonely.

Valentine (1)

Its tail is tiny.
It hasn't got claws.
Its fur's rather shiny,
And though it lacks paws,
It certainly knows how to frolic and play.
So yours is the pussy for Valentine's Day.

Valentine (2)

I'd still like to versify this valentine,
Even though I can't make it scan or rhyme.
I keep on churning out drafts, but it's little use
Now I'm off the visiting list of the Muse.
Erato's well aware of who has my heart,
Yet she continues to expect a card.

Down with the Dove

I feel constricted by my love,
Because it fits me like a glove.
So now I think I'll give a shove,
And burst the stitches of my love.

Playtime

Boys and girls, come out to play,
The lads with lasses – unless they're gay.
Leave your console and leave your crack:
It's fun in the sun till your parents get back.

Come with a whoop,
Come with a bawl,
Come with abandon:
That's best of all.

A Norfolk Romeo

Oh! It's sixteen miles to Swaffham,
And the fairest of the fair.
Yes! It's sixteen miles to Swaffham,
But my heart's already there.

If I ever get to Swaffham,
And her father bars the door,
Well, I'll cycle home to Fak'nham,
But I shan't go back no more.

Multiple Personality

Bilbo is a silly goose:
Thinks his collar is a noose.

Bilbo is a greedy pig:
Wants his bowlfuls nice and big.

Bilbo is a crafty fox:
Gets through doors in spite of locks.*

Bilbo is a timid mouse:
Much too shy to find a spouse.

Bilbo is a lucky dog:
Life's like falling off a log.

Bilbo is a basking snake:
Hard to tell if he's awake.

Bilbo is a gentle lamb:
When he bites it's just a sham.

Bilbo is a wise old owl:
Likes to snooze before a prowl.

Bilbo's this and Bilbo's that,
But he's very much a cat.

*via a cat-flap

Privileged

Petra knows some special gardens,
Which she's shown to lucky me.
One's not far from where she lives now:
At its heart a bench and tree.

Petra liked to sit and read there,
Partly shaded from the sun.
Then some yob who found this haven
Sprayed graffiti just for fun.

One's at Vauxhall near the Oval,
Hidden in a pretty square.
Those who own it tend it wisely:
Shrubs and flowers prosper there.

When this garden's nearly empty,
On a bench on which we've sat,
Up will jump the watchful keeper:
Such a solemn little cat.

As it happens one's wherever
Petra finds herself to be.
Others have to pay to enter,
Unlike lucky, lucky me.

Well Done! Wexford

The gateposts seen in Ireland
Are mostly tall and square,
With pointy bits on top of them
That stick up in the air.
But Wexford posts have rounded shafts:
They do things better there.

Verses for Someone in Rehab

1.   You say you're OK down below. In bed
           Maintain it well and stop it running dry.
           But up above's important , too. Your head
           And heart are what I mean. You can't deny
           You'll need them both in working order when
           It's time to cope with city life again.

2.   He: I've kept my promise to you, Love.

           She: But how can I know?

           He: Just look at my hands:
                I've let my fingernails grow.

Restricted Area

The angels flap and fold their wings
To keep the little fiends at bay.
But Petra's flaps and folds are things
That never, never bar my way.

The Happy Eater

Whenever I felt peckish in my prime,
I liked to gorge in Soho a la carte.
But now home-cooking triumphs every time.
An expert in the culinary art
Lives quietly not far from Bounds Green Road,
And I prefer to feast at <u>her</u> abode.

Dental Surgery Rag

Oh! Dentist, use your skills to ease my pain.
Without some help from you I'll go insane.
I rub it, but that twinge keeps coming back.
A torturer has got me on the rack.

Now just relax, lie back, and open wide;
Then let me slip this instrument inside.
My expertise is bound to do the trick.
We'll have you feeling better double quick.

Oh! Thank you, clever dentist, now I'm calm.
Your knack and knowhow worked just like a charm.
I've so much confidence in your technique,
My next appointment's got to be this week.

On the Job

The plumber's bag is crammed with many things,
But not the stuff that, as a rule, he brings:
An altar candle, food for cats, blue soap,
A bunch of summer flowers and perhaps
A neatly folded hankie. Can he cope?
How <u>will</u> he fix the drains and faulty taps?
He won't. Those blockages and leaks must wait.
The plumber's come to see the plumber's mate.

A Vagina's Monologue

I thought our rights would also be respected,
Once Women's Lib was up and riding high,
But now I'm feeling downright disaffected;
So listen comrades, let me tell you why.

According to the feminist agenda,
Despite the Latin meaning of our name,
In future all possessors of pudenda
Would bare their bits with pride instead of shame.

How dim we were to heed this propaganda,
Believing that the world would soon play fair.
We should have sussed our owners' lack of candour
About their attitude to what's down there.

They place their mirrors carefully below them;
Then, fidgeting to get a better view,
They anxiously consider what these show them:
Their labia, are they slightly on the skew?

That puckering, could it be unattractive?
The cladding of their clit seems rather bold.
Their surgeon, though, is eagerly proactive,
When asked to match a porno centrefold.

Oh! Comrades, this is not what I expected;
The sisterhood has made us all look fools.
The privacy of privates is rejected,
But now cosmetic mutilation rules.

The Rake's Ingress

She's a sluttish old hussy,
Who presumes he's not fussy.
It may well be clapped out,
But her pussy's not pussy.

Plumbing <u>and</u> Heating

The plumber's been to nightschool now
And learnt another trade.
With extra skills to offer
There's more money to be made.

His most rewarding service, though,
Is one he offers free:
To Powerflush the hot-pipes
Of that mate he goes to see.

The Horny Lepidopterist

Whoever said
That yours, when spread,
Reminded him of one of these,
Deserved the look
He fondly took:
Such compliments must surely please.

Regression

Boobs are for babies;
Minges for men.
If he can't get it in,
Let him suckle again.

Evolution and Mrs Darwin

Those lumps of sun-bleached driftwood that were picked up
on the shore,
And specimens of seaweed taken home for study; or
Assorted fossil fragments put on permanent display:
Each one is full of interest in its own distinctive way.

For probing nature's secrets it may offer subtle hints;
As candy for the mind's eye it's as flavoursome as mints.
Whatever its appeal, though, to a science or the Muse,
There's seldom any balance in its contours, planes and hues.

The symmetry of faces and proportionment of limbs
Are gifts from evolution that it didn't make to quims.
An upright walk worked better if the quim was tucked away.
Then modesty made certain it was rarely on display.

So, unlike limbs and faces, where men's thirst for beauty tends
To ditch what's deemed unsightly for whatever least offends,
The quim remained quite wayward in respect of its design:
No pressing need for beauty, so no pressure to refine.

But what about an era well acquainted with their form:
As time went by might quims perhaps evolve towards a norm?
With webcam sex a gogo and explicit DVDs,
Could outre variations, though efficient, cease to please?

Then quims would lose their likeness to formations shaped by
chance,
Becoming standard fitments that a surgeon might enhance.
Your time's up, sports of nature; here's your cue, genetic strife.
Conformity may conquer thanks to bias – and the knife.

Lovebane

Obscenity claims just one noun
Still more or less taboo.
Some say it's such an ugly word,
But is this really true?
'Punt', 'cant' or 'curt; 'hunt', 'Kent' or 'cult':
Are these words ugly, too?

There's ugliness in some men's minds:
A very baneful brew.
It saturates their thoughts on sex,
Which fester, through and through,
Infecting these men's acts of love,
No matter what they do.

Sildenafil Stomp

When I looked and saw him slyly pop that pill,
The yummy letch I had for him turned rancid.
If he did want sex (he plainly wasn't ill),
No way could it be little me he fancied.

Reaching back and crossly doing up my bra,
'You're not turned on one bit by me,' I grumbled.
'Bugger off and try to find your bloody car.
And mind that unlit walkway where you stumbled.'

'Though it's true,' he said, 'I've brewer's droop tonight,
It's you I fancy, pet: you don't half send me.
And the stuff won't work without an appetite.'
I caved in then, although he did offend me.

Having billed and cooed for half an hour or so,
They're both relieved to see what's on display now.
The great Satch then blows a brisk Stomp off, Let's go.
That bright blue pill has chased the blues away now.

The Experts

Looks seldom trump the need to be
At ease with one another.
I can't relax when friends agree
She's very like my mother.

And will she try to play the tart,
Predacious, pierced and painty;
Or hinder progress at the start
With efforts to be dainty?

From thoughts like these my feeling grows:
We humans need new teachers.
There's much to learn from bonobos*
As well as other creatures.

---

*I followed the seventh edition (2005) of <u>Collins English Dictionary</u>, which put the stress on the first syllable, and was, I think, the first British dictionary to include the word. But in speech this seems to have settled down now, possibly under American influence, with the stress on the second syllable.

Foreplay <u>then</u> Wordplay

A long-forgotten marriage guide
For those with elementary schooling,
Though rather on the wordy side,
Contained an estimable ruling.

The carnal pact of wedded life
Shall lay on men this stipulation:
If you're aroused, arouse your wife
With digital manipulation.

One wonders what they made of this,
The handbook's band of earnest readers,
But hopes it led to seemly bliss,
With wives as lovers, not just breeders.

Their own descendants, eyes aglow,
Show all the signs of deep entrancement.
That rapt expression means they know
The joy of digital enhancement.

Self-Help

I like a girl who looks after herself;
I like a girl who can frig without fuss;
I like a girl who conveys what she wants:
Then there's less down-time for either of us.

Threesome

There's a go-ahead girl called Miss Hook,
Who unwinds in a sheltering nook.
She's perfected this habit
With some help from a rabbit
And a foxily readable book.

Lament

'Look! She's cross.' The speaker pointed at her bushy tail
Swishing like the feather duster of a saucy maid.
'No, she's not,' I said. 'It's joie de vivre. That furry flail
Seldom rests. It's what she waves to welcome the parade.

'When she's putting guests at ease, she wags it – like a dog.
Come to think of it, that's not her only canine trait.
Suppertime? She looks me in the eye and, all agog,
Leads me to the kitchen, where, before she eats, we play.

'Hide and seek is quite good fun, but hurts my dodgy knee.
Ready, Steady, Go she calls in this soprano bark
Unlike standard feline sounds. I'm sure you'll all agree
Meows and purrs are not for her. The contrast's pretty stark.'

Now she's gone. A seizure, blindness, then the handicap
Mounting lameness meant for her. Yet still she soldiered on:
Relished food and made her own way out of doors to nap.
Tuesday was good company, a friend. But now she's gone.

Love's Labours

What once was scruffy waste has since been turned
By Petra into garden. There she's dug
A pond and grows the plants for which she yearned,
Protecting them with care from weed and slug.
Inside her flat the massive door she hung
Had thwarted all the landlord's handymen;
And now she climbs her ladder rung by rung
To make the indoor paintwork fresh again.
If Petra's up, her working day's begun,
Which means that, braced by many mugs of tea,
She'll persevere until a job is done,
Yet in between jobs still have time for me:
   Not just at night, when only half awake,
   But in the sunshine by a glinting lake.

Am I Normal?

'Completely normal, all of them,' the doctor reassures,
As, thoughtfully, a group of youngsters – boys and girls – inspects
Two photographic line-ups of contrasted private parts.
These are, it seems, all free from anatomical defects,
Unblemished by the signs of an embarrassing disease,
And fully fit to carry out their reproductive task.

Yet here are youngsters entering the rat-race of the genes:
What bearing has all this on what they'd really like to ask?
OK, they aren't deformed, but did they ever think they were?
Perhaps they're just uncertain whether theirs will truly please,
Fulfil a lover's expectations, deepen the rapport.
Such things, though, lie outside the doctor's field of expertise.

Epitaph

Stone-deaf, stiff-limbed, unkempt, ill-clad, her coat a knotty mat,
She kept her self-respect and status: Flo the alpha cat.

Size Matters (Sampling <u>My Secret Life</u>)

When Walter turns from reportage to broader observation,
This man of action <u>and</u> voyeur makes use of tabulation.
In brief, his data bear upon the size of an erection:
A bit below six inches is the average projection,
And Walter doesn't <u>say</u> that his extends beyond this figure.
Ah! Gentle reader, had you pictured something rather bigger?
But those who revel in what's rude, unroused by what's romantic,
Can all relax, because they'll find his index is gigantic.

Ellie: In Memoriam

Lost and scared till you found our place,
Making it your home.
Ten snug years with a private space:
No more need to roam.

Then you went on a walkabout,
Never to return.
Tall black cat, did your luck run out?
Too late now to learn.

Death of a Hero

With short white fur and probing bright-blue eyes
Our Baggins was a charismatic cat.
Keen-eared (he wasn't deaf) to match his sight,
He had no time for sitting on the mat.

Defined by roads that Baggins had to cross,
Twin territories formed his massive realm,
Each isolated by the urban sea;
Two ships of state on which he took the helm.

He had his pick of low-born girls on heat,
An active ladies' man despite the snip,
Though etiquette ensured he'd also hump
The alpha queen on boarding either ship.

One night the boss was busy on his rounds,
But roadhogs see a cat as just a cat.
Another moving target in his sights,
The driver didn't brake, and that was that.

The Dog Lovers

When Phyllis feels like having sex,
She gets down on all fours.
Her partner, Paddy, wags his tail
And grips her with his paws.

When Daisy does it doggie-style,
It's Trevor's special treat.
He has a choice of entrances;
She knows that's up his street.

But Phyllis fancies Daisy too
And shows this in her talk.
She'd love to do it girl on girl.
The boys could take a walk.

The Mug that Cheers

There are treatments intended to bring you relief,
When you feel at the end of your tether.
But hot Bovril's a drink that will brighten your day,
When you're just a <u>bit</u> under the weather.

Why?

I've given way to deep despair,
Now women shave their pubic hair.
If hosting crabs is what they dread,
Can nits still populate their head?
Or have they all dreamt up a fate:
To be some paedo's gaolbait?
A nuisance, then, they can't ignore,
Their pubic hair is shown the door.
To me, though (and some other men?),
It's grassland round a hidden glen.

In empty pits where hair once grew,
I picture smaller meadows too.

Tuesday II

Let's all encourage her theatrical demeanour:
Up on her hind legs like a pointing ballerina.
Whenever meals are almost ready, in she prances.
Instead of singing for her supper, Tuesday dances.

Smile!

Sadly, week after week,
The near future looks bleak:
Just a string of ordeals, not adventures.
There'll be less of this pain
And you'll smile once again,
When you're wearing your cutting-edge dentures.

.

In Praise of Promiscuous Women

I like girls who take life in their stride.
Girls who've made their playground planetwide.
Girls whose golden rule is laissez-faire.
Girls who'll rendezvous no matter where.
Girls whose thoughts won't dwell on who you are.
Girls whose pants don't always match their bra.
Girls who'll blithely marry blue and pink.
Girls who don't care tuppence <u>what</u> you think.
Girls who keep some condoms in their bag.
Girls who hand one out before a shag.